THE SNACK SNEAK

THE SNACK SNEAK

Logic Games, Mysteries and Quests

written by
Carol Ledden

illustrated by
Chum McLeod

Annick Press Ltd.
Toronto, Ontario

Editor: Jane Lind
Design: Brian Bean

Annick Press Ltd.

Annick Press gratefully acknowledges the support of the Canada Council and the Ontario Arts Council.

Canadian Cataloguing in Publication Data

Ledden, Carol, 1964 –
   The snack sneak, logic games, mysteries and quests

ISBN 1-55.37-332-3

1. Educational games.   2. Group games.   3. Games.
I. McLeod, Chum.   II. Lind, Jane.   III. Title.

LB1029.G3L44 1993   371.3'97   C93-094105-5

The art in this book was rendered in pen and ink. The text has been set in Bookman and Franklin Gothic by Attic Typesetting Inc.

Distributed in Canada by:
Firefly Books Ltd.
250 Sparks Avenue
Willowdale, Ontario   M2H 2S4

Distributed in the U.S.A. by:
Firefly Books (U.S.) Inc.
P.O. Box 1325
Ellicott Station
Buffalo, New York   14205

∞ Printed on acid-free paper.

Printed and bound in Canada by Webcom Limited

For the Love family as I knew
them—Melanie, Christopher, Gerri
and Billy—who invited me into their
home and didn't get upset when the
kids and I messed up the house,
playing.

 You encouraged me to keep
learning and stay "silly."

Thanks.

A resource book for people who work with groups of school-age children, or those who like to plan games for kids.

contents

introduction

Answering riddles, finding treasures, discovering clues and solving puzzles – why are these activities so compelling to both children and adults?

For one thing, they give us a sense of pride, confidence and intelligence, while exciting us with mystery and adventure. Also, they let us share a secret and be part of a group. Like a good joke, mysteries and puzzles do not have to be long, but they should make us smile and feel good, so that we will remember them and then tell someone else.

I remember playing logic games as a child with my family at the dinner table, on car trips, and while camping. Then, one Easter, we found notes with clues to help us find hidden eggs. These extra clues made our egg hunt much more exciting. My parents, however, should have made a list of the hiding places, because throughout that year we found old melted chocolate eggs that we had missed that Easter morning. We had the mystery egg hunt only once, but I will remember the excitement of it my whole life.

I have been working with groups of children for many years in camp settings, day-care centres and homes. My experiences have taught me that planning and playing mystery games with children is a great way to get them excited about working together.

The adventures, mysteries and quests in this book involve action and fantasy as well as logic. Logic challenges can help develop and promote skills in language, math, reading, writing, sequential thinking, communication, exploration of ideas, and abstract thinking. Sound like a lot? Well, it is! The more opportunities we can provide for facilitating positive self-concepts, the better.

Do not worry about children being too old or too young. From "Peek-A-Boo" to mystery dinner theatre, logic games and mysteries are popular. The following list should not be used as a rigid guide, but I have noticed many times that:

Three-year-olds want magical things to happen, and like treasures and treats.

Four-year-olds often like to look for things: hidden treasure or missing toys.

Five-year-olds may enjoy fantasy stories – visiting six-foot rabbits or secret elves.

Six-year-olds enjoy clues, solving crimes and working with friends.

Seven-year-olds may like dinosaur adventures, alien landings, or disguises.

Eight-year-olds often like to play detective, be challenged physically and hunt for answers.

Nine-year-olds may want to have longer, more technical challenges, or plan games themselves.

It is important to be organized when preparing for a mystery game or quest. As your planning abilities increase, so will your children's problem-solving abilities. Give your children the information they will need for solving the puzzles and pursuing the clues that you will be putting into your game. Play short games when you begin. Gradually, try longer and more elaborate ones.

Creating predictable signals for mystery games helps children feel safe in pretending and knowing when you are play-acting. For example, they may learn that every Friday something "silly" happens, or perhaps they discover a big "?" on the calendar signalling a mystery game on a given day. At Brant Street Daycare we have a regular spot where notes are hidden: up the nose of "Fertilizer Face," as we call him, a three-and-a-half-foot papier-mâché mask on the wall. When we find notes there, the children know a game is starting.

You can use this book not only for the games explained here, but as a resource for ideas to create your own. You can also adapt the games to suit the children you work with, or to play at home. Some of the games are, in fact, designed to be played at home (for example, "Where's Teddy?").

So read through the book, choose the games that excite you and give them a try. Get tricky, get silly and plan a game. There are all sorts of ways to keep adventure in play – it never has to stop.

about the Snack Sneak

The staff and kids at Brant Street Daycare in Toronto have been solving mysteries for the past five years. We are a school-age day-care centre serving more than 50 children in a school-based programme. The mysteries started with the Snack Sneak, a mythical prankster who hid our special Friday snack and left only clues or a trail to follow. Our younger school-age group loved the excitement and anticipation of finding a clue with the Snack Sneak's recognizable symbol. They began telling stories and creating a background and history for the mysterious figure. Sometimes we would find a balloon with a secret coded message inside, or the Snack Sneak's chalk symbol left on the playground.

I do not know if the Snack Sneak is male or female. I do know that it likes to play games, leave notes, hide toys and generally disrupt our routine with play.

THE SNACK SNEAK'S STEAL

steal #1

Hello, reader. So, you want to try out some of my games, eh? My friends and I would love to visit, taunt and tease you.

Well, I'll start you off simply. I can make your snack time a little more active and a lot more fun!

I'll use a school-age day-care setting, since that's where I've sneaked the most snacks from.

The Game Begins

A staff person and two children innocently go to the fridge to get this week's special Friday snack.

Inside the fridge they find a big note on colourful paper marked with the famous "X," but no snack.

The staff member embellishes:

"Oh no! It looks like our snack is gone! We'd better go tell the others!"

The adult and the kids return to the group, bringing the note with them. Read the note to the whole group:

> Hello, my friends, let's play a game. Check your room for the same.
> —The Snack Sneak

Show every one the note with the "X" symbol.

Solution: *More notes are hidden in the room.*

14

Naturally the kids are upset that the snack is gone and they start searching the room for more notes with "X" marked on them. They find six more notes that you have discreetly hidden around the room beforehand.

Note 1: [hidden under a table]

Note 2: [hidden inside the closet door]

Note 3: [hidden high on a wall]

Note 4: [hidden under a chair]

Note 5: [hidden under a couch cushion]

Note 6: e [hidden in the drama centre]

Each note should have the "X" on one side and a letter on the other.

Direct the kids to look for clues and to find the hidden messages. Bring the clues together and write them on the blackboard, or tape them to a wall.

They will have to unscramble the word "office."

In an excited yet orderly fashion, everyone goes to the office. Open the door and find the snack with a note from "X" saying,

> **Congratulations, you've done well. Next time may be more difficult, but when it is, I'll never tell.**
> **—The Snack Sneak**

Finally, everyone can eat the snack.

What You Will Need

- Time to hide the notes before the game
- First Snack Sneak note (hidden in fridge)
- Six notes (as outlined above)
- Final Snack Sneak note (in office)
- Snack (in office)
- Co-operative adults, ready to play
- A group of hungry kids

After-the-Game Discussion

- Who is the Snack Sneak?
- Why did he/she/it take the snack?
- Will he/she do it again?
- Will it be harder to find next time?
- Do we want the Snack Sneak to come back?

KEY GAMES

Key games have a code or secret "key" that you must unlock to find the solution. Usually, one or two people who know the key to the game demonstrate it to others and invite them to figure out how the game works. It is important for everyone to be included, and "get it." So, let the participants discover the key for themselves, remembering that these games require creative thinking, communication, and observation skills.

Purple Magic

In this game, two players tell their audience that they can communicate by magic, Purple Magic. Player A leaves the room while the audience picks an object. Upon her return, Player B asks questions of Player A and "magically" communicates what object was picked.

The audience's job is to figure out how the information was communicated. Was it magic or not?

The Game Begins

Start with two people who know the "key" (Player A and Player B), plus an audience of one or more (good for classrooms, living rooms and dinner tables).

Player A leaves the room.

Player B says to the audience: "We know how to communicate by using special magical powers, and I can transmit my thoughts to [name of partner]. Pick any object in the room and I will let my partner know which object you picked."

Invite people to figure out how the communication is carried out. What is the key?

- Someone picks an object: the red scarf.
- Player A returns to the room.
- Player B says, "Is it...the blue book?" (any object in the room that is not purple)
- Player A says, "No."
- Player B repeats "Is it...?" (you can repeat this stage many times) or says "Is it...the purple poster?"

(must be something purple)
- Player A says, "No."
- Player B says, "Is it the red scarf?" (The correct object is chosen only after a PURPLE object has been picked.)
- Player A says, "Yes, of course it is."
Ta Da!

Key: *it is always the object selected **after** a purple object*

Rainbow Magic

Change the colour of the key and follow the same format as above.

Alphabet Magic

Spell out the object with the first letters of the words that you have chosen to point out. (For example: Is it the coat? No. Is it the apple? No. Is it the table? No. Then what is it? The Cat. For long words, the first key player may have guessed the object before the other has finished spelling it.)

Howling Wolf Club

In this game we are inviting the audience to join our club, but they must repeat the initiation procedure, which usually has a subtle key that people often miss, exactly as demonstrated.

The Game Begins
One "key" player and the audience are the players. (This game is good

for classrooms, dining tables and living rooms.)

The "key" player says to the audience: "I have a club and I want you to join, but you must complete the initiation and do what I do."

The "key" player clears her throat.

"The wolf has two eyes, a long snout, sharp teeth and a cunning wit."

(Make gestures in the air using your finger as a pen, drawing the snout and spots for the eyes, and point to your own brain for the cunning wit. Then give a howl.)

Now the "key" player chooses people to perform the initiation ritual and join the club. If they follow the directions exactly (throat clearing, hand gestures, words and howl), welcome them into the club and have them demonstrate the words and gestures with you. If they do not follow the initiation, say "That was very good, but not exactly what we need. I hope you will try again, because I'd really like you to be in my club."

Key: *Clear your throat before speaking.*

Star Club

For younger children, follow the game above, but use a verse from the song "Twinkle, Twinkle, Little Star" (or something else they already know) and create hand gestures to match, folding your

hands at the end.

Key: *Fold your hands at the end.*

Galaxy Club

For older children, use the pattern of the "Howling Wolf Club," but substitute the planets in our solar system (Mercury, Venus, Mars etc.), with gestures to match. Clear the throat in the beginning and add a head-scratch in the middle and folded hands at the end.

Key: *Clear your throat, scratch your head and fold your hands at the end.*

Adapting the "Club" games

Additional "keys" for variations:
- pushing up your shirt sleeves
- smoothing your skirt, or shirt
- looking at your watch
- crossing and uncrossing your legs
- brushing at your ear lobe
- putting your hand behind your back
- looking behind you
- scratching your leg

Have fun making up all sorts of clubs, and see how complicated the subtle signals can become.

Magic Counting Sticks

In this game, two "key" players explain and demonstrate that magic sticks can represent the numbers from one to ten, and you will invite people to understand how to read the magic sticks.

The Game Begins

You need two "key" players and an audience. The first key player is an observer and does not reveal that she knows the key.

The second key player says to the audience, "Did you know that with four different kinds of sticks we can magically form the numbers from one to ten?" Explain that a very readable pattern will emerge and if they are attentive they will see it too. Prove to the audience that it is true by getting four types of "sticks" (ruler, pen, straw, spoon, etc.).

Have the audience form a circle, or make sure in some other way that they can all see the surface where you will throw the sticks. Throw the sticks randomly onto the floor and look at them intently. With your hands by your legs, or otherwise discreetly visible, indicate the number by the number of fingers you are showing.

Then ask, "Who knows what number this is?"

The first "key" player gives the answer (however many fingers the second "key" player is showing).

Everyone will be looking at the sticks, trying to figure out how the first key player knew this.

Ask someone else to throw down the sticks, but keep showing what the number is by signalling it with your fingers and responding positively to correct guesses. Remember to encourage other guessers and exaggerate movements to let players in on the secret.

Key: *The number of fingers showing on your hands.*

Adapting the "Magic Counting Sticks" Game

To help them concentrate, have younger children use only two similar magic sticks (two pencils, etc.), and only go up to the number five. Always keep your hand in the same position, in plain view.

Key: *the number of fingers showing on one hand.*

For older children, increase the difficulty of the math by using the left hand for tens and the right hand for the ones, as in sign language.

Key: *the number represented by the fingers on your hand.*

THE PASSING OF THE STICKS

For these games the children sit in a circle on the floor.

Explain that the sticks can be passed to one another, and that it shows great strength to know how to read the passings.

Crossed or Uncrossed

The Game Begins

Taking two sticks, the key player, sitting with legs crossed, says "I receive these crossed..." Now the key player uncrosses the legs and says, "... and pass them uncrossed."

Other players tell how they have received the sticks and how they passed them. The key player and other players who have it figured out should correct the passers as each takes a turn. Remember to exaggerate movements and give clues to the key of the game. Our intention is to include other players.

The players are watching the sticks and each other for the clues to this game, when they will find the answer is really with themselves.

Key: *Are your legs crossed or uncrossed when receiving and passing the sticks?*

Growing Sticks

The Game Begins

The "key" player says, "I receive the sticks long and pass them short."

The player who passed the sticks has long sleeves, and the player the sticks are passed to has short sleeves.

Key: *Observe the sleeves of those on either side. Are they long or short?*

Adapting the "Growing Sticks" Game

Use any characteristics of the children or their appearance as keys for passing the sticks.

WHERE'S TEDDY?

a bedtime mystery

In this game, a parent and child play hide-and-seek together with a stuffed toy. (Ensure that your child will not be frightened that Teddy is *really* missing. Explain that you are playing a game, that Teddy has permission from you to be hiding and that no one should go off hiding without parental permission.) In this example, we will follow Grace, a six-year-old girl, and her parent (you), who is getting her ready for bed.

The Game Begins

When Grace goes up to her room with you for bedtime stories, she will find a card on her pillow from her stuffed bear, Teddy. You and Grace read the card together.

"Dear Grace: Let's play hide-and-seek! Love, Teddy. P.S. – Look around your room for my pawprint."

Grace looks around the room and finds pawprints on her mirror, with a very small note attached: "Look where you sometimes pretend to swim."

You and Grace go into the washroom and find a pawprint on a balloon hanging from the tap in the bathtub. Inside the balloon is a note. Grace breaks the balloon and unfolds the note, which reads:

"Now that I'm clean, I feel sort of hungry."

You and Grace go to the kitchen to find an empty glass that Teddy has obviously been drinking from. (It has more pawprints on it.) There is a note under it which says, "Keep looking!"

Grace finds two other pawprints and notes; one is in the fridge and one is by the cookies.

1) The note in the fridge says "KETS."

2) The note by the cookies says "BLAN."

You and Grace realize that the notes together spell the word "blankets."

You go to where the blankets are stored and find Teddy hidden under them. He is holding one last card.

It reads: "I'm so glad you found me, I knew that you would. Now I'm tired, can we go to bed? Love, Teddy."

What You Will Need

- A china marker (to make pawprints on glass; alternatively, you can use a soap bar to make markings on glass surfaces that can be wiped off later)
- A stuffed toy that your child will notice is missing
- Small paper and pen for making the notes
- Tape
- Balloon and string
- Two cards from Teddy
- Time to place the clues without being seen
- An emptied glass of milk

Adapting the Game

For children who cannot read, make the notes with pictures. Use as the last notes two halves of a drawing of the linen closet or laundry. If your child does not have a bear, use any stuffed toy. Some families might not want to play this type of game so close to bedtime; try engineering a walk in the early afternoon, when you casually ask "Grace" to bring her bear along.

THE SNACK SNEAK'S CODES

I love sending my messages in code. It drives people crazy!
Number codes are my favourite: there's so much variety! Here are some for you to try.

Using codes can add all sorts of fun to lunch box notes or messages on the blackboard. Make up blank decoding charts so you can create your own codes.

They can be simple translation codes, or more complicated cryptograms. Word-based codes can be simplified to colour- and shape-based codes for players who cannot read.

The use of codes develops skills in language, recording, math and observation.

Number Code A

A/2	B/	C/6	D/8	E/10
F/	G/14	H/	I/	J/20
K/	L/24	M/26	N/25	O/
P/21	Q/19	R/17	S/	T/13
U/11	V/	W/7	X/5	Y/3
Z/1				

Solution: Z = 1, A = 2, Y = 3, B = 4, etc.

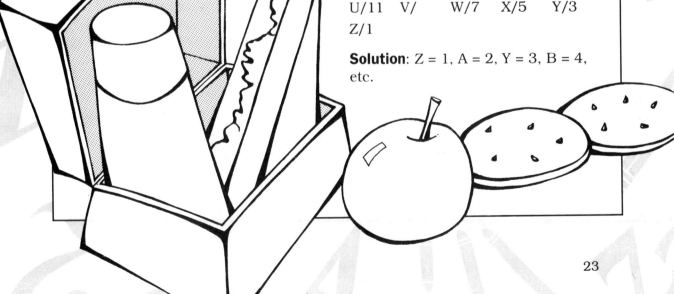

23

Fill in the missing numbers; using the decoding chart, translate the message below.

7,16,2,13   7,10,18,14,16,15
26,23,17,10,   2
21,23,11,25,8   23,12
24,10,2,8   23,17   2
21,23,11,25,8   23,12
12,10,2,13,16,10,17,15?

Answer: 25,10,18,13,16,10,17.

Number Code B

A/1	B/4	C/7	D/11
E/14	F/17	G/41	H/44
I/47	J/71	K/74	L/77
M/111	N/114	O/117	P/141
Q/144	R/	S/	T/
U/	V/	W/	X/417
Y/441	Z/444		

Key: Starting with A=1, use numbers made up of only straight lines.

Why not send out your next party invitations in code? If you really want to bug your friends, send the decoding chart a few days later.

Other languages can be used as codes. Have French, Spanish or other translation books available.

Finger Spelling Chart

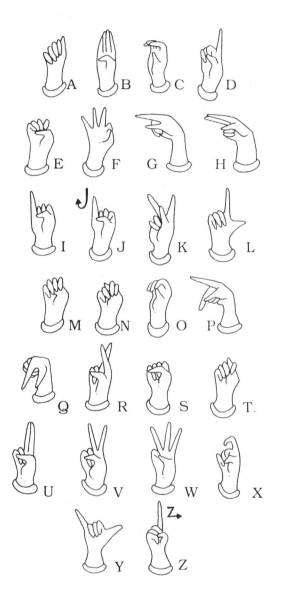

Backwards Writing

elttil gniyonna na tsuJ•
.rehpiced ot uoy rof elddir

elddiR

)duola gnus ro dias eb oT(

•You're driving a bus.

•At the first stop, 5 people

get on.

•At the second stop, 3

people get on and 4 get off.

•At the next stop, 2 people

get on and 1 gets off.

•Now here's the question.

•Who is driving the bus?

•Don't you hate this kind

of riddle?

Key: *The riddle is just written backwards.*

Word-Based Codes

Code 1

Before time did Georgina and you create and figure math problems it never played out?

Key: *Read every third word.*

Code 2

The Hat Eats Snake News And Cake Kisses Silly Nifty Elephant And Kisses Igloos Stupidly. Giant Reptiles Eat All Toothbrushes!

Key: *Write the first letter of every word.*

Code 3

If dogs you love haven't gone noticed missing by late now, maybe I don't like you to always play silly tricks. Careful if now you breath are not observant then you never will easily find briefly a short mystery cleverly spread here throughout after this odd book. Beautifully, It's not my planned special taped message given to all you, foolish but sports good bad luck for finding but it.

Key: *Read every other word.*

Reflection Writings

Reflection writings can be easily read when seen in a mirror. Writing them may take some practice; remember to write from right to left, not left to right!

A B C D E F G H I J K L M
N O P Q R S T U V W X Y Z

HOW MANY LETTERS IN THE ALPHABET DID NOT NEED TO BE REFLECTED?

Ways to use reflective writings:

- Messages in balloons
- Notes in children's lunch boxes
- Jokes for party favours
- Clues in mystery games
- Riddles from the tooth fairy

THE SNACK SNEAK RETURNS steal #2

So, you're ready for another of my games, are you? Let's use the same unsuspecting staff and kids. Tell them to go to the kitchen for their special Friday snack, which I have snuck once again!

The Game Begins

The staff person accidentally turns out the kitchen light, and the group finds an acetate sheet with glow-in-the-dark writing on it.

The note reads:

> Guess who's back! That's right, it's me, the Snack Sneak, wanting to play some more. If you're not hungry, why don't you go run around for a while?

(The clue is written with glow-in-the-dark paint, which will need the light beforehand to make it glow. Make sure all the curtains are closed to make the writing look brighter.)

One staff member should be ready ahead of time so that the group can quickly go outside to the playground.

The kids and staff members, once in the playground, look around and spot Xs marked in chalk, on the ground, in a trail. The trail is made up of Xs, but at some points messages say "Clap your hands," "Jump on one foot," or "Yell, 'I love you, Snack Sneak.'" Everyone should follow the trail, which will lead across the street and into the park.

In the park there are bags of popcorn hanging from the trees, each marked with an "X." There should be enough for every child and adult. Each bag also contains a personal note from the Snack Sneak, written on a peel-and-see clue card. (See page 46 peel-and-see instructions.)

Suggestions for peel-and-see messages:

> Well, my clever friends, you found the snack again. I cannot eat your food, but it smells so good, I can't help having a little fun by hiding it on you. I may sneak your snack again, so be careful. As a reward for finding it, look under the sticker to see your fortune.

Under the stickers write little fortunes, such as:

- You will grow tonight.
- You will get a mysterious phone call.
- You are loved.
- You will find some money.

Or make up nasty ones, such as:

- You will pick your nose.
- You will get dirty.
- You will dream of pickles.

What You Will Need

- Kids and staff
- Time and privacy to set out hanging bags of popcorn (this could perhaps be done by a volunteer parent or an older child)
- A sheet of acetate (available in stationery stores)
- Glow-in-the-dark paint or marker
- A dark kitchen (or other room) where you can pretend to have left the snack
- Chalk, and trail in chalk on pavement
- A park (or somewhere else the trail can lead)
- Bags of popcorn
- String or thread (dental floss works well for hanging up popcorn bags)
- Peel-and-see cards—markers, stickers, fortunes

SNEAKY RIDDLES

Riddles seem to be passed down from generation to generation. Here is a selection of riddles, old and new. Many different answers could be applied to most of them.

Confusing you gives me such joy! Just like mystery games, riddles are my toy.

The Baker

(To be said or sung aloud.)

Once there was a baker who dreamed of a pie,
she dreamed of a pie, one hundred in the sky.
Once there was a baker who dreamed of a cake,
so on the next day, a dozen she did make.
Once there was a baker who dreamed of some tarts,
seven lovely tarts, that she never did start.
Once there was a baker who counted up her wares.
How many baked goods did she find there?

Solution: *twelve or thirteen (thirteen = a baker's dozen)*

The Park

On a very hot summer's day, Cindy went out for a walk with Amiel. They stopped by the park and played frisbee all afternoon. Amiel and Cindy were both tired and thirsty,

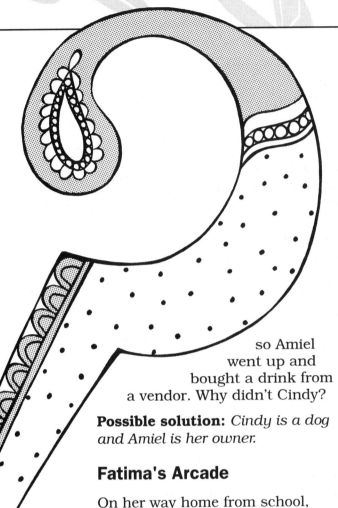

so Amiel went up and bought a drink from a vendor. Why didn't Cindy?

Possible solution: *Cindy is a dog and Amiel is her owner.*

Fatima's Arcade

On her way home from school, Fatima noticed a new video arcade across the street, above a record store. It was very attractive and she had heard some of the other kids at school talking about it, but she continued on her way home, without going in. Why?

Possible solution: *Fatima is in a wheelchair, and since there was a staircase instead of a ramp, this arcade was not accessible to her; or perhaps she had left her money at home.*

The Women on the Bench

Maria and Louisa were sitting on a bench. Another woman walked by.

Maria said to Louisa, "That woman's mother is my mother's only daughter."

Who was the woman walking by?

Solution: *Maria's daughter. (Idea from Beverly Sobers)*

The Cottage

Cathy and Mario went up the hill to the cottage they were staying at for the summer.

When they got there they unpacked their bags, put on suntan lotion and found a place outside to relax and read. Normally, they both read just before going to bed, but during this trip they didn't.

Why?

Possible solution: *They had no candles and the cottage had no electricity.*

The False Robbery

One day, Martha phoned the police, telling them to come over right away. When they got there, she told them that someone had robbed her. She said, "I was on the street coming home from a walk when I saw a light on in my living room. I went up to the window, but couldn't see in very well– it was so cold, and the window was all frosted up– so I scratched the frost off with my nails. All I could see were two people just leaving the room, so I ran and called the police. They stole all my good things!"

The police knew Martha was lying. How did they know?

Possible Solution: *Frost would form only on the inside of the window panes. (Idea from Martha Scroggie)*

The Dance on the Hill

A teenager named Dominque was on his way to the top of a hill where a celebration dance was happening. He was very late and it was getting dark. On his way he passed three men and waved to them. Farther on, Dominque passed what appeared to be a group of seven young women. It was so dark now that he could not make out their faces. He did, however, notice that each woman seemed to have a sleepy child holding onto each of her hands. Dominque continued on his way.

How many people were going to the dance? Hmmm...

Possible solution: *only one, Dominque; the others were leaving, which is why he passed them. (Variation on the old St. Ives riddle)*

The Best Haircut in Town

Omar, who was new in town, wanted to get his hair trimmed.

There were only two places to get a haircut in this town, both just across the street from one another. On the north side of the street was Simone's Clip and Snip; when Omar looked in the window, he noticed that Simone had a bad haircut. On the south side of the street, at Mark the Barber, he saw that Mark's hair looked great. Omar went to Simone's Clip and Snip. Why?

Possible Solution: *If Mark went to Simone's and he looked great, why shouldn't Omar?*

Fred and Ethel

When I came home from work one afternoon, I was shocked and saddened to see the bodies of Fred and Ethel lying, dead, upon the floor.

They were lying in a pool of water, the window was open, and there was some broken glass.

What happened?

Possible Solution: *Fred and Ethel were fish whose bowl had been knocked over by something that came through the window. (From an old fish tail)*

OLD BEAR'S GHOSTLY CASE

a
mystery

In this game, a stuffed toy or a puppet receives a message from an old relative (Old Bear) who has died and left behind a mystery. It is Old Bear, who is now a ghost, who wants an old crime to be solved. The game starts when the children find a manilla envelope containing a cassette tape, a code puzzle and clue notes to be followed. (Notes 1, 2, 3, 4 and 5 will lead to notes A, B and C.) By following the notes and clues, the children solve the mystery and discover a map leading to Old Bear's treasure.

This mystery is intended for groups of six to eight children, seven to twelve years old, with reading skills. It is ideal for an after-school programme or for a sleep-over party. You can play too, so if the children are going in the wrong direction, let them. Steer them back subtly if they get too frustrated, but usually the difficult challenges are the ones children enjoy most.

The Game Begins

A favourite stuffed toy (bear, in this case) is discovered holding a manilla envelope. On it is written: "PRIVATE and CONFIDENTIAL. For Bear and friends, to be opened [today's date]." The kids find that the envelope contains a cassette and a file of some old drawings and notes.

The "detective" group listens to

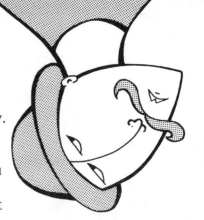

the tape and hears Old Bear's story.

"To my niece, Bear, and her friends. You will be hearing this long after my death, but I hope you all remember me fondly. You should all be old enough and smart enough now to help me solve a mystery that I never did figure out while I was alive. Before any of you were born, I was robbed. Two items including a beautiful watch that my father had given me were stolen. I got the watch back, but I never did figure out who took it. I had my suspicions though, and raised such a fuss that I think I frightened that crook into giving me back the watch. One thing that was never returned was a treasure box that I had filled with special things. If you do figure out who took my stuff, maybe you will discover where they hid the treasure too. Well, good luck! I left all of my notes and drawings to get you started, and I will do all I can from wherever I am. Do not forget me now."

After listening to the tape, the group sorts through the pictures and notes and begins to make sense of them. The group starts "detecting."

In the file, they find:

Pictures (drawings of suspects outlined below)

Suspect #1 BIG TOE VAUGHAN – Black hat, blue shirt, and glasses

Suspect #2 STEAMING RACHEL – Black hat, yellow top, and glasses

Suspect #3 SLOPPY JOE – Black hat, yellow top, mole on face and moustache

Suspect #4 GINGER ALE BURB GINNY – Black hat, blue shirt, and moustache

Suspect #5 WRONG WAY SEAN – Black hat, blue top, mole on face, and glasses

Notes

Note #1

e g d i r f

Solution: *The scrambled word is "fridge;" hide note A in the fridge.*

Note # 2

h o c u c

Solution: *The scrambled word is "couch;" hide Note B under a couch cushion.*

Note #3

- Found glasses by the couch and the next day they were gone.
- My watch was returned to me on the table.
- Saw Rachel looking through the window.
- Saw Wrong Way pulling at the curtains.
- Saw Joe staring at the fridge.

Note #4

d o w W i n

The scrambled word is "window;" Note C is behind the curtain.

Note #5

This is a decoding chart with parts missing.

A/65	B/55	C/45	D/35	E/25
F/15	G/05	H/94	I/84	J/74
K/64	L/54	M/	N/	O/
P/	Q/	R/	S/83	T/73
U/63	V/53	W/43	X/33	Y/23
Z/13				

(Code solution: if Z=31 (which is 13 backwards,) and Y=32 (which is 23 backwards), can you figure out the rest? Missing numbers are M/44 N/34 O/24 P/14 Q/04 R/93)

By following Notes 1, 2, 3, 4, & 5, the group discovers Notes A, B and C.

Note A

To Handle Every Month All People In Silly Islands Not Time Hours Every Day. Islands Can Take It On Naturally After Red, Yellow Umbrellas Nearly Die. Everything Read May Yield No Adventure. Mustard Elephants.

(This note is in code. Use only the first letter of each word: the note will read "The map is in the dictionary under my name.")

Solution: *Look under "B," for Bear*

Note B

Journal

Monday – I saw someone with a blue top following me to the dentist.

Tuesday – Today I saw someone with glasses following me.

Wednesday – I saw someone with glasses at my window.

Thursday – Someone with a mole was in every store I went to today.

Friday – There were two people following me; one wore a yellow shirt.

Saturday – Someone with a moustache was outside my window.

Sunday – Someone tried to steal my shopping bag. Something about the face looked familiar.

Monday – I think the person who tried to grab my bag was the same person I saw on Thursday.

Tuesday – This morning, someone in a blue shirt ran away from my door at 3 a.m. I also found my watch tonight!

Wednesday – I found a broken pair of glasses and all my things were upside down.

Note C

Turtles Hardly Ever Make Apple Pie In Sisters Underwear, Not During Egg Raids. Alligators Don't Easily Skip Karate.

(This note is in the same code as the previous one. It will read "The map is under a desk.")

The "detectives" can use the pictures and notes to make some deductions and search for the map pieces.

The Map

Draw a map with directions written in code. Tear the map in two, hiding one section in the dictionary under B and the other section under a desk. The "detectives" must find the map pieces, put them together, and follow the map, which will lead them to the treasure.

You will need to create your own map, but here is an example.

Instructions, using note #5

43/65/54/64 65/93/24/63/34/35 73/94/25 55/63/84/54/35/84/34/05 73/94/93/25/25 73/84/44/25/83. 74/93/24/44 73/94/25 05/23/44 35/24/24/93, 73/65/64/25 73/25/34 54/65/93/05/25 83/73/25/14/83 73/24/43/65/93/35 73/94/25 83/54/84/35/25. 34/24/43 35/84/05.

Solution: *Walk around the building three times. From the gym door, take ten large steps toward the slide. Now dig [would be our sand area].*

34

(The treasure should be buried under something such as sand in a playground or blankets in a laundry room.)

The Treasure

The children uncover a buried container: the treasure!

I recommend a non-sugar snack such as popcorn, and/or inexpensive toys such as decks of cards. (A shoe box could contain treats, comic books, disguises, mini flashlights or anything else you can come up with.)

Inside the container you can have one last note from Old Bear, written from beyond the grave.

How to set up the game

What You Will Need

- Stuffed toy (the "niece")
- Large manilla envelope
- Blank cassette and tape recorder
- Actor to be the voice of Old Bear
- Pictures/drawings of suspects
- Notes with clues and cards with clues (use firm sturdy paper that stands up to handling.)
- Map
- Place to bury treasure
- Treasure and container
- Time to hide clues
- Six or seven interested kids

Presentation means a great deal. Make your clues easy to read and you could burn the edges of the maps for that "aged" look. Decorate a cardboard box for the treasure, or wrap up the treasure in dark cloth and tie it with string or ribbon.

Making the Tape

In your recording, it is best to use a voice the children will not recognize. Adapt the wording to

make it more personal, mentioning the kids by name if you know exactly who will be present for the game. (If you have a VCR and recorder, you may want to try using videotape.)

Hiding the Clues

Hide your clues carefully an hour or so before the game, or earlier, if possible. To ensure that no one finds anything ahead of time, hide your clues so that they cannot be seen unless someone looks underneath something. The clues will direct the players to look in specific spaces, so the setup should not be too simple. I have never had clues missed yet, although some may have needed adult prompting.

Making the Pictures

Many people say they cannot draw. You probably can, but if you absolutely do not want to, use a photocopy or cutouts. Advertisements work well because you can probably get all the cutouts you need in just a few magazines. Also, cut-and-paste work looks mysterious. If you use this technique, photocopy the criminals' names along with incriminating evidence.

Working Together

Co-operation and discussion are the really important aspects of this game. Allow discussion of clues and suspects to range in many directions. There is no need to be correct. If the detectives come up with a different criminal, great!

Give them enough space to work in, so that everyone can see the "evidence." Tape the clues up on the walls; write down the children's solutions. When it is time to follow the map and find the treasure, make sure everyone is together.

Adapting the Game

If the clues outlined do not fit into your setting, change them. You can easily change the "fridge" unscrambled clue to something else in your setting, such as "table."

If the clues are too difficult for your children's ability level, simplify them by removing the coding or using only one map. For an extended game, or when playing with a larger group, you can add more paths and challenges for the children to solve.

If you think the topic is upsetting to young children, change it to Bear's Reward, and the theme is that Bear is just playing a game.

"CHALLENGE" GAMES

These are group games requiring some sort of physical accomplishment from the players.

These "challenges," like many of the other games in this book, have no right or wrong answers.

There are guidelines to be followed, but many possible solutions.

They can be as easy or difficult, as silly or serious, as you like. Often these "challenges" help to focus attention and promote trust within groups, and develop creative problem-solving, decision-making and leadership.

On the grass or in the snow, here's a slimy game for you and your kids to try.

Back Worms

Mark starting and finishing points at least twenty metres apart. You can use chalk or lay a skipping rope on the ground.

The players form a line at the starting point, everyone facing backwards. Each player puts his/ her hands on the shoulders of the person in front.

The Challenge: The "worm," i.e., the column of players, must travel the length of the course without breaking the connection. If any player's arm should separate from the person in front, that player must make the separation complete and leave the "tail" of the worm wherever it is on the course.

The front part of the worm continues to the finish line, but then must return, connecting en route with the back of its tail, which now becomes the front. The "worm" finishes the course as a whole.

You can make it even tougher: extend the trail to a greater length and add obstacles for the worm to manoeuvre around, through, over and under (such as tires, swings, bridges, etc.).

Now that you have your kids working as a team, try some other "challenges."

Reach the Mark

Using chalk on a wall (or a taped-up piece of paper), draw the shape of a hand, or any other shape big enough for a hand to fit inside. Place the mark higher than any individual in the group can jump.

The Challenge: All players must touch one palm to the spot on the wall.
Possible solutions: Players could piggy-back one another, go and get a ladder, or form a human climbing-apparatus.

You can repeat these challenges, trying to improve the group's co-ordination and timing. Observe the amount of time needed, what methods the kids come up with, and whether patterns emerge. Knowing they will get to face the same challenge again can help build confidence, and the children may plan ahead of time for this week's "Reach the Mark."

Crossing the River

Mark two "river beds" on the ground, at least two metres apart. (Coloured chalk on pavement looks great! You can even put in fish, or, for wider rivers, include stepping stones.)

The Challenge: All players must cross the river at least once without getting wet.
Possible solutions: Players could build a boat or a bridge, or carry each other across.

People Pretzel!

This game has had many "campers" all mixed up for years, but it never loses its twisted sense of humour.

For a group of all ages.

Everyone should stand fairly close together and raise one hand. Using the hand that is in the air, each player finds another person's to hold; everyone should still have one hand free. Each player raises the remaining free hand in the air and finds another hand (make sure they are holding two different people's hands). If you want to make it difficult, go under someone's leg or over and through arms to find your second hand-holding partner. Now your group is a big tangled people-pretzel.

The Challenge: Holding hands gently but firmly (no letting-go, but allowing room to manoeuvre), untangle your pretzel. This game should always work out. Sometimes you may get one large circle (with some people facing in different directions), or you may get a few circles, just by chance, of different people holding hands within a smaller group. Either way, untangling the mess is fun!

SECRET FRIENDS
an interactive mail-mystery

In this game, children (with some reading and writing skills) from different schools or day-care centres set up a mystery for each other. Each student will have a secret friend to write to, but the children are not allowed to reveal their names. The notes are to be written in code. Each child has a counterpart, so no one is left out. The purpose of the game is to guess who is writing to whom. (All the children will go by a code name to receive the correct mail.)

Children love to receive mail, and in this game everyone who participates receives at least five letters. At the end, the children meet new people and have a chance to make new friends. The game also develops reading and writing skills.

As a group, the children also learn about the mail system, and can make a chart to see if delivery schedules change or vary, depending on where things are mailed. This can be a project carried out in conjunction with another school or day-care centre in the same town or even in another country.

Co-operation among the teaching staff is needed, and the game should be timed so that on a school holiday, which would be a full day for school-age day-care

centres, the two groups can have a chance to meet. Also, the teachers will need to help co-ordinate the matching of "secret friends" so that no one is left out. The children must possess reading and writing skills if you want them to have independent communi cation.

The Game Begins

Invite the children to play a mystery game with another day-care centre.

The older kids at Brant Street Daycare wrote to the kids at Fashion Ryerson Daycare, and the children ranged in age from six to ten years old. Some were able to write independently and others needed assistance with letter writing.

Decorate a bulletin board with displays, use a map to show where the mail is coming from, make a chart of the children's secret friends and what facts are known about them (for example, he's a boy, has freckles, and likes kick ball). By monitoring the game's progress on a bulletin board, you are encouraging discussion and communication, as well as practising different recording techniques.

Keep a calendar posted to show when the secret friends will get a chance to meet. Plan a joint activity day and invite the other day-care group over to a park.

One group should mail letters first. Decide with the teachers of the other day-care centre which group will do the first mailing. Record by code name who is writing to whom so that you can co-ordinate the exchange of letters. For example: Eggplant received Hyena's letter.

Have the children sign up and make a commitment to the game. When you have your groups, you and the staff person in the other centre can match up children and give out game kits. Remember to notify parents about the activity.

Game Kits

- Five or six envelopes and postage stamps
- Writing paper
- A code name
- An address– either home, school, or day-care centre
- A special pen for writing
- A photocopy of a class picture
- Code chart papers (the alphabet written out but the codes not filled in yet)

A/	B/	C/	D/	E/
F/	G/	H/	I/	J/
K/	L/	M/	N/	O/
P/	Q/	R/	S/	T/
U/	V/	W/	X/	Y/
Z/				

If your group has not worked with codes before, hand out some samples and explain how they work.

Letter #1

All secret friends will write their first letter, and address it to "My Secret Friend." The letter should include a photocopy of the class picture, a decoding chart, instructions for playing the game and a note written in code. Without revealing their real names, the children can give information about themselves.

In each letter, secret friends can ask "yes" or "no" questions about the photo, or tell things about themselves. (For example: "Are you wearing a dress? Are you standing beside someone taller than you? Are you smiling in the picture?" Or, "I like baseball. What do you like?")

Letter #2

By now everyone should have received mail. The writing back and forth should continue, with each secret friend asking "yes" or "no" questions about the other one. By using the photocopy as a guide, the children might already be guessing who their secret friends are.

They could start including other little things in their letters, such as drawings, stories or poems.

Talk about the mail the children have received and keep the display board up-to-date.

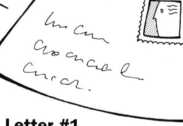

Letter #3

Have people guessed identities? Remind the children to write in code, and keep them corresponding; getting to know one another through letters can take some time.

Letter #4

By this point the children know quite a bit about each other. Now it is time to exchange names and phone numbers. The secret friends can arrange for a time to call and speak with one another.

Letter #5

This is the last letter before the secret friends meet face to face.
You can ask them:

- Do you know what your friend's favourite foods are?
- Will you continue writing?

The Meeting Day

Begin with some organized activities to break the ice (see list below). Teachers should have this co-ordinated so that a part of the day is in a non-structured setting, allowing children the chance to get to know one another. Some might want to go off and sit in the swings talking, others might want to play soccer, etc. Children who did not sign up for the secret-friend mail will also benefit from meeting new children.

Some suggestions for organized games are:

- Dress-up relays
- Water-balloon tossing
- Co-operative baseball (no teams–positions just rotate)
- Obstacle course games
- Trust games
- Skipping
- Parachute games (a king-size sheet works too)
- Co-operative tag
- Physical "Challenge" games

If the day goes well, you may want to plan other activities or trips together. It is a great way to save money when hiring performers, and gives everyone another chance to interact with the larger community.

SNEAKY TRICKS

Want to be sneaky like me? Try out this trick on your kids, then show them how to fool their friends!

I Know What You Are Thinking!

A magician (you) invites a friend into her room and says,

"I have a magic trick to show you. Pick a planet in our solar system, but don't tell me what it is." The player thinks of one and tells you so.

You say, "Write it down, just to be sure." You give her pen and paper, but do not touch the paper, so it doesn't look like you're cheating.

Pretend to think really hard. Think harder. Now tell your friend that you are ready too!

Ask, "What's your planet?" Your friend will think you have blown the trick and tell you "Mars" (or whatever).

You say, "That's what I thought. Go and look under the vase on the table."

There your friend finds a similar piece of paper, folded up, with the word "Mars" printed on it.

TA DA!

Here is how it works.

To get ready, leave eleven pieces of folded paper around the room, each with the name of one planet written on it: Mercury, Venus, Earth, Mars, Jupiter,

44

remember. Or how about matching the planets to a hiding place that starts with the same letter? e.g., Venus = vase or Mars = mat, etc.)

When your player has chosen a planet, tell her to look in the place where she will find the note with the name of her planet.

Pretty sneaky, eh? It's an oldy, but a goody.

Here are some tricky ways to leave clues or send messages with an element of surprise or mystery about them. Having to uncover something adds an element of fun to clues. Remember to test them out before using them in a game.

Scratch-and-See-Cards

These cards are like scratch-and-win, but instead of winning money, you are exposing a clue or puzzle piece.

Write a clue or message on the card, using a red pencil. Cover the area that you do not want exposed with black crayon. Be careful not to cover up too much; black crayon can be messy.

Make a sample first to see how well it works. Different paper and different crayons may work better than others. In very humid weather the paper tends to absorb the wax, so it is hard to scrape it off without tearing the clue.

Saturn, Uranus, Neptune and Pluto. There are only nine planets, so write out the moon and the sun, too. Memorize the locations and what planet is in each location. (If you leave them in the order of their distance from the sun, they may be easier to

What You Will Need

- Black wax crayon
- White index cards
- Red pencil crayon (or red pen)

Why not leave a message in your child's lunch, or match up class project partners using clue cards?

Peel-and-See-Cards

These are similar to scratch-and-see, but instead of covering the clues with wax crayon, you cover them with stickers.

What You Will Need

- Colourful circular stickers (most stationery stores have them for colour-coding files)
- Cards or paper with a slight gloss (this makes it easy to peel the sticker off)
- Markers

Be sure to test out your cards. Some stickers do not peel well with certain kinds of paper. You can cover up jokes or riddle answers, or send a peel-and-see card in the mail.

SECRET WRITINGS

Your kids can leave each other notes, making sure you cannot read them!

Lemon Juice Writings

Using a small paint brush, cotton swab or toothpick, write your note with lemon juice.

When the lemon juices dries it is barely visible, but when the paper is "toasted" (carefully), the lemon juice darkens and the message becomes visible. Some people use candles to warm the paper, but toaster ovens or light bulbs are safer and easier to monitor.

What You Will Need

- Lemon juice (concentrate works well)
- Plain blank bond paper (try all sorts, though)
- Thin paint brush, cotton swab or toothpick (although toothpicks can be frustrating)
- Toaster oven, lamp or candle

Magic Wax Writings

By writing with a white candle (you must press hard, just as you do with a wax crayon), you can leave a secret message that is clearly visible only after you lightly paint the paper with water colours. This is the same process as wax relief painting, or crayon resist. It is also a great way to leave clues, but add instructions so the players know what to do.

What You Will Need

- White wax candle (birthday candles will do, but are hard to work with and break easily)
- White paper (coloured paper will not work, because the wax must not show)
- Water colour paints and brush

Imprinting

Just like people in the detective movies, you can scribble lightly (with soft pencil) on a piece of paper to see what the person before you wrote.

Use a pen, with the lid on, to write a note on a pad. The person needing to read your clue must do a pencil rubbing on the sheet in order to see your message clearly.

What You Will Need

- Pen with lid (remember to press hard)
- Pad of paper
- Soft pencil for rubbing

Be mischievous! Next time you send a card, sign it only with your imprint.

THE SNACK SNEAK'S ATTACK

steal #3

The Game Begins

A staff member and (correctly suspicious) children once again go to get their special Friday snack. Inside the freezer they find a note with the now-famous X, and they excitedly bring it back for the group to read.

The note reads:

> Well, my friends, your snack looked so tasty I just couldn't help hiding it. Are you up for a game? Are you up to a code? We'll see.

The Coded Message

Frogs In Riddle Stop To Go Every Time. Indoors Now, Time Will Open Gates Round Our Umbrella Purple Sides.

Green Red Orange Ugly Pineapples On Never Eggs– Silly Hot Olives Under Love Dinosaurs Specially Every Evening Kangaroos On Ugly Tables. Twice Huge Elephants Ostriches Nearly Leaked Yellow. On New Elves With Happy Old Restaurants Over All Mushrooms Slowly. Tidy Hair Evens Whales Homes Over Land. Every Skate Can Hold Olives, Only Loosely.

Green Red Orange Ugly Pineapples Twinkle White Olds– Gizzards On Top Of Tight Hair,

Eggs Even Lean Down Every Step Tomorrow. Friday Orange Rainbows May Over Ride Every Inch Now Formed On Red Marches And Tie Igloos On Nests.

Key: *Pick out the first letter of each word. Decoded, the note should read:*
First get into two groups. Group one should seek out the only one who roams the whole school. Group two go to the eldest for more information.

Riddle answers:
Group one– the caretaker
Group two– the eldest staff member
   (You should have a group-separation method ready for dividing the kids quickly and fairly. Remember to spread out children with different skill levels.)
   Group one hunts out the caretaker, who very co-operatively has a note stuck to the bottom of his shoe. (However, he should not give it up too easily.)
   The note reads:

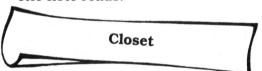

In the closet, the group finds a balloon with a note inside.
   The note reads:

> *Good work. Now build up your appetite a bit by going outside by the slide.*

Inside the slide is another note; it reads:

> *After everyone has had a turn on the slide I suppose you will be ready for your snack, so go back to where you began– the day-care room! Ha ha!*

Group two finds the eldest staff member (you can have different clues if people are sensitive about their age).
   This person also has a note taped to the bottom of the shoe which she should not give up too easily. The note reads:

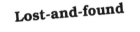

At the lost-and-found box, a balloon is hidden inside. There is a note inside the balloon which reads,

> *Good work, my friends, but you are not done yet. Go outside and run around the baseball diamond.*

At the baseball diamond they find another note, folded and marked,

> **Do not open until all of you have run around the track.**

Inside, the note reads,

> **You all did well. I suppose you are ready now, so go back to where you began. The day-care room! Ha ha!**

In the day-care room you have their snack laid out, with the final note on the chalkboard.

> **Got ya!**
> **—The Snack Sneak**

What You Will Need

- The same co-operative staff and volunteers
- Caretaker with a note
- Eldest staff member with a note
- Someone to set out the snack after the kids have gone on their hunt
- A co-ordinated plan to supervise transitions (having one adult go with each group, or an adult stationed in all the different areas that the groups will be visiting, works well)
- Note in fridge, large enough to be taped on the wall for the whole group to see
- Chalkboard for writing out the solution to the first note
- A snack for the detectives' return
- Group one clues:
  - Caretaker's note
  - Balloon in closet and note
  - Note in slide
- Group two clues
  - Eldest staff member's note
  - Balloon and note in the lost-and-found
  - Baseball diamond note

Adapting the Game

You can make this game easier, or longer and more difficult. If you do not want to use food, have the Sneak swipe and hide something else. With the older kids at Brant, he/she/it has started hiding their favourite toys. I suppose it was tired of sneaking snacks all the time.

THE BALLOON BANDIT

This is an indoor/outdoor birthday mystery for young investigators, ages five to seven years. They will need some reading skills, or an adult to help with the introductory clues.

In this game, the children will discover balloons where there was once a table loaded with birthday presents. (It is important to have the children prepared so that they do not become upset when the presents go missing.)

The Game Begins

You announce that it is time to go and open presents, but when you and the children return to the room where the presents were, you find balloons and a very big birthday card instead.

The card reads:

Ahh! So it's your birthday and all your friends have brought you presents. Well, my gift to you is a game, and if you are very smart and your friends help, maybe you will find your presents and get them all back.

The Balloon Bandit

P.S. Kids– if you want to help your friend, pick one balloon and look for another one of the same colour.

There is one balloon for each child; you can attach name cards to the balloons (instead of following

51

colour). Each child breaks her balloon by any means (stepping or sitting on it, for example) to get at the clue inside. (This is a good game for recreation rooms, or back yards.)

In this example we will use only six children, but the game can be adapted for much larger groups by having more than one child follow each colour.

First child– blue balloon – paper has a picture of a tree – in tree, blue balloon – paper is a piece of a puzzle picture.

Second child– red balloon – paper has picture of garden shed – in garden shed, red balloon – paper is a piece of a puzzle picture.

Third child– green balloon – paper has a picture of a garbage can – in garbage can, green balloon – paper is a piece of a puzzle picture.

Fourth child– pink balloon – paper has a picture of a bush – in bush, pink balloon – paper is a piece of a puzzle picture.

Fifth child– yellow balloon – paper has picture of a fence – at fence, yellow balloon – paper is a piece of a puzzle picture.

Sixth child– purple balloon – paper has a picture of a back doorway – in doorway, purple balloon – paper is a piece of a puzzle picture.

When the children have followed their clues, they put the puzzle pieces together and see a picture of a couch. Everyone returns to the living room and finds all the presents hidden under the couch. They solved the mystery and should be thanked by the host for all their help. This may be a good time to give out the loot bags as a reward! (See page 61)

What You Will Need

- Balloons
- Notes– clue cards
- Markers for making the clues
- Drawing of a couch (to cut into pieces)
- String and tape for hiding the clues
- Some time to set things up

Adapting the Game

Remember to change things to suit your situation. If you do not have a couch, find a better hiding spot and draw that as your puzzle picture. If it is winter, you will probably want to change some of the details for the sake of convenience.

How about sending out puzzle pieces for a party notice instead of the whole invitation at once, or send out the birthday invitations in code, and make mysteries the theme for the day.

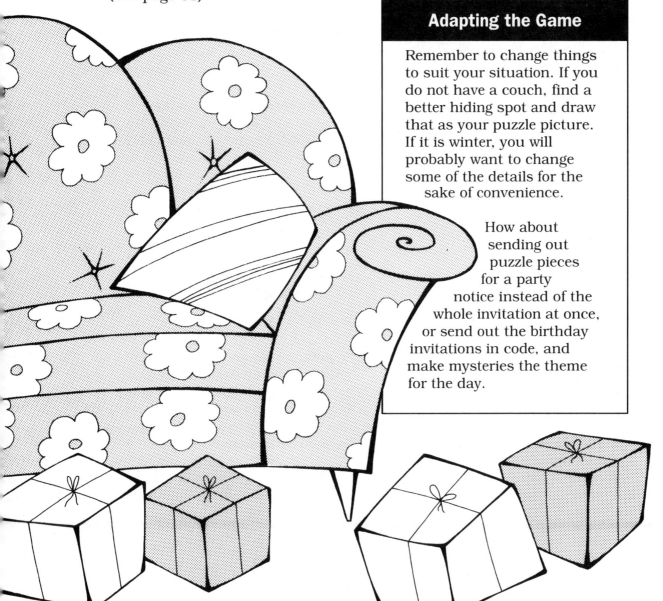

SNEAKY TALES – "what if?" games

These are sneaky tales to start you off... but you have to come up with the endings.

This game leads people to hypothesize, pretend, communicate and interact. The group is given a starting sentence or two, and then must come up with the ending, continuation or explanation.

"What If?" games can be played anywhere by any number of people. All you need is a starting scenario and the players go from there, adding the rest in a way that makes sense to them.

Try to steer the group into coming to logical conclusions, but if none can be found, so be it. There is no right or wrong in these games. They provide practice in sharing information and the giving and receiving of feedback.

Some Sample Beginnings

What if a photographer went into a store to buy some film for his camera, and the security alarm went off when he opened the door?

What if a clown named Bobo lived in a trailer with five dogs and two birds and, one day after an extremely exciting circus act, Bobo went back to the trailer to lie down and never got up again?

What if a boy named Mohammed, who lived with his brother and mother in a house near his school, one day found a million-dollar lottery ticket while walking home?

What if a girl named Aquisha had special powers and could talk to the animals where she worked at the zoo, but one day the leopard went missing?

Remember that "What If?" stories can go in any direction, fantastical or practical. It's all great pretending.

What if you woke up one morning, wishing you were invisible, and discovered that you were?

What if your dog came up to you and said, "I think we need to talk"?

What if Reema came home from work one day and found all her furniture up on her roof?

What if Jun-chao drove to the airport to pick up her aunt visiting from Hong Kong, but when she arrived, noticed her old aunt leaving with someone else?

What if you were watching the stars one night, and saw a UFO?

What if you were late for school one day, and as you ran to get there on time, discovered you could fly?

55

In most of these games, children work in detective teams on different "Top Secret Assignments." Generally, the assignments involve a little detection and a lot of dramatic play.

Crime Lab

Set up a crime lab in your drama area.

R.C.M.P. INVESTIGATORS

What You Will Need:

- Instamatic camera and tripod
- Chalkboard background for line-up shoot
- Blank "Wanted" posters
- Pretend crime rap sheets
- Bulletin boards for displaying photo line-ups
- Map of your neighbourhood and pins for marking
- File folders marked "Top Secret"
- Index cards
- Phony ID
- Markers/pens/pencils
- Fingerprint kit (see below)
- Disguise kit
- Table and chairs for work area
- Display area

You can participate, too: interview suspects, be a witness, take photos or record the facts. When the kids are familiar with the equipment and ready for specific assignments, hand over (or keep on display) the Top Secret Assignment Files, or play "Who did what?" Detecting can be done in pairs. I usually have only two investigating teams out at once; this means less confusion and more detection, especially since some missions require "security clearance" (meaning the kids need permission to travel between rooms). Have each assignment brightly labelled in a file folder, so that when the mission is accomplished it can be redone by a different investigating team.

Crime Lab Assignments

Top Secret Assignment Example #1

Security Clearance Required: Must get permission from teacher to visit other day-care rooms to interview suspects.

Your mission: One of the staff members is living with a five-pound, sharp-toothed, hairy beast! Find out where the beast lives, its name and what it looks like. Make a poster of the beast for your files.

Suspects: All the day-care teachers and the caretaker.

Warning: Do not alert suspects! Be careful with your questioning techniques.

Top Secret Assignment Example #2

Your mission: One of the teachers has an alias and is now using a different name. Find out who the teacher is, what the alias is and where he/she lives. Once this is discovered, get it confirmed.

Note: Agents must use caution; do not alert suspects.

Clue: You may need to consult the phone book if suspects are stubborn.

Suspects: Adults in the day-care room.

[Choose a suspect who owns a particular household pet. A rabbit perhaps?]

[Choose a suspect who uses her married name; the address can be looked up in the phone book.]

The purpose of these missions is to have the children come up with creative ways of solving problems and accomplishing specific tasks– and to have fun going around with badges, questioning people. The missions can be complicated or simple. Try to get the children using resources for information, such as finding definitions or looking up authors.

You can create a whole series of secret missions based on a language programme or book. Ask questions such as:

- Who was the author?
- Where does the author live?
- Who was the illustrator?
- Who are the main characters in the book?

Who Did What?

A photo crime lab game.

In this game, the children will be criminal photographers and play an ever-changing "Whodunnit?" game, using the photos and false crimes they create.

The Game Begins

Set up a picture-taking area, and do photo line-ups. (A chalkboard is a good background. You can draw lines to show height.) Have name-plates for the kids and staff to hold, including identification number and criminal name, real or alias. Display the photos on a bulletin board so they can all be seen easily.

On index cards, create a file of names (the same names used in photos) and a file of crimes. Make them silly; keep it light-hearted.

Suggestions for crime file

- Barking illegally
- Break and deny
- Stealing home base
- Blue jay walking
- Walking over the speed limit
- Driving without a car
- Failure to stoop and scoop
- Taking in the garbage
- Composting on public property

Solving the Crimes

Two players are needed, one a witness and one a detective.

The witness pulls a card from the "names" file, and the detective pulls a card from the "crimes" file. The witness should have time to look at the board to see the criminal (allow them 30 seconds). Then the detective interviews the witness, explaining what crime was committed.

The detective may interview the witness for as long as necessary, but may ask only "yes" or "no" questions to figure out who committed the crime.

When the crime has been solved, it is listed on the back of the criminal's card.

Props for Detectives

ID Badges

Make cardboard cutouts and cover them with aluminum foil. Try using business-card-size boards or heavy paper, and laminate them. Cut an old chequebook holder in half to use for a badge holder. Use school photos of your children in the badges or ID cards. Clear plastic bank-book holders are great for making false ID seem more real.

Disguise Kits

- False moustaches (the ones with sticky tape work best)
- Badges or identity cards (store-bought or homemade)
- Scarves (used for all sorts of purposes)
- Eyeglasses (take out the lenses) and sunglasses
- A pipe (Sherlock-style, or corncob)
- Hats (look for soft hats that will not require a hat box and can be washed)
- A cape (any piece of thin, dark material) and a safety pin for a fastener
- Costume jewellery
- Simple, water-based makeup
- Soft wax for making scars (the wax coating from some cheeses works well)
- Baby powder, poured into a sock you can use like a big powder puff (applied to the hair, it makes you look old and grey)
- Triangular bandages for "patients" look
- Canes, umbrellas, etc.

Detection and Fingerprint Kit

- ID badges (police, detective, FBI, RCMP, etc.)
- Magnifying glass
- Stamp pad (for fingerprinting)
- Cards (for fingerprinting)
- Clear plastic bags (for clues and evidence)
- Large, soft makeup brush (for fingerprint dusting)
- Small container of baby powder (fingerprint dust)
- Clear, wide, sticky tape (for lifting fingerprints)
- Writing tablet and pens (for collecting information)
- Instamatic camera and film
- White labels (for identifying objects in bags)
- Old file folders (for storing information)
- Tape recorder and tape cassettes (dictaphones work well, and are small)

I just couldn't keep away. So, to help get you in a criminal mood, try setting up "silly" crimes.

Silly Crimes

Make up "Wanted" posters for criminals and have "silly" crimes.

Use magazine cutouts with real or fictitious names. For example,

Wanted: Slimy Fingers Sam
Known criminal, wanted for questioning in connection with the theft of five cents from the two million dollar man.

Record: Found guilty of putting away dirty dishes without washing them.
Found guilty of wiping his nose on his sister's sleeve.
Found guilty of burping in bed.

Remember to falsely accuse the kids and staff in your centre or home. Just for fun, put them on mock trial too. If you still want to play, here is a birthday party idea for junior sneaks!

Mystery Loot Bags

- ID badges (make your own and have them laminated, if you can)
- Mini fingerprint kit (small brush, pieces of clear tape or stickers, small vial of baby powder, small bags with labels)
- Small stamp pad (for fingerprints)
- Stamp reading "Top Secret" or "Private"
- Small magnifying glass
- Small spiral-bound note book and pens
- Scratch-and-see kit (black crayon, red pencil crayon, small white cards)
- Blank "Wanted" poster
- Code book containing examples and some blank code sheets

Think of more things you could include.

THE SECRET VISITOR
another mail mystery

Everyone loves to receive mail; it makes us feel special and important. This goes for children as well, who normally receive mail only at holidays.

In this game, a child receives mysterious mail full of puzzles and riddles from "the secret visitor." In the example used below, Luke, a seven-year-old boy, is receiving mail from his grandpa. All Luke knows is that the letter writer will be coming to visit his family, but his parents are keeping the visitor's identity a secret. Luke will follow the clues to figure out who "the secret visitor" is.

The Game Begins

Find a picture of "the secret visitor" and get it enlarged. (Find a photocopy machine that is capable of making enlargements.) Cut the enlargement into pieces and mail one out every few days with a note. Use fancy, coloured envelopes, or mark them with question marks, so Luke recognizes that another piece of the puzzle has arrived. Also, to make it even more special, you could seal the notes with wax and a stamp. You will need to adapt the clues to suit your situation.

If you are making the clues and letters on behalf of the visitor, someone else who will be visiting your child, you can prepare everything ahead of time, ready to be mailed out at intervals.

The child should receive a piece of mail every four or five days. Each letter is to include a different puzzle piece and a short note. Save the puzzle pieces that have the eyes on them for the end– they are a give-away.

Note #1 [example]
Hello, Luke. In three weeks you will be having a visitor to your house.

I thought we'd play a game to see if you can figure out who I am.

Save these clues– you will need them later. I will be sending you more clues to my identity; you can ask your mom and dad for help, but not to give away the secret. They're playing along and have promised not to tell, so you'll have to figure it out for yourself.

They told me what a great detective you are. I wish you good luck!

— —— —— ————

_____.

A I M F A L I N I Y U O Y R M

(*unscrambled, this sentence reads: I am in your family*)

Note #2 [example]
[On one side of a card is the message, on the other side is a chart.]

Side A

Hello, Luke.

Did you figure out the last clue? Well, here's another one for you.

26/25   16/2/18/11   18/13
14/11/10/25,   18/15/13
3/5/15   2   21/18/14.   26/25
24/5/19/10   12/5/11   25/5/17
18/13   19/10/11/25   4/18/14!

Side B

A/2	B/4	C/6	D/8	E/10
F/12	G/14	H/16	I/18	J/20
K/22	L/24	M/26	N/3	O/5
P/7	Q/9	R/11	S/13	T/15
U/17	V/19	W/21	X/23	Y/25
Z/1				

Solution: *My hair is grey, it's not a wig. My love for you is very big!*

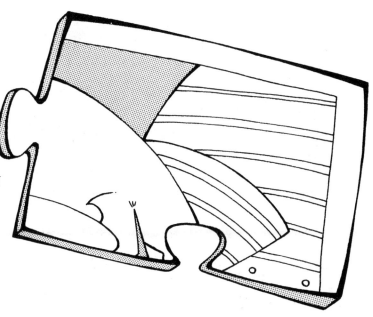

Note #3 Example

Have you guessed who I am yet?

   If you think you know, ask your parents for permission to call and find out, but I may fib just to keep you guessing!

Note #4 Example

Hello, again!

   It's almost time for me to come. Have you figured it out?

   You call me a name that has seven letters.

__ __ __ __ __ __ __

Solution: *Grandpa*

Note #5 Example

Well, Luke, this will be my last clue. Soon you and your parents will be picking me up from the airport. I will have flown a long way to see you.

   Did you check the postmark to see where I'm coming from?

   By this time, Luke should have all the puzzle pieces and should have solved the secret visitor game.

What You Will Need:

- Blown-up photo or drawing of the secret visitor (to be cut up like a puzzle, with different pieces sent out at different times)
- Five notes containing clues
- Five envelopes
- Five postage stamps
- Markers, stickers, etc. (to decorate envelopes with)
- Wax sealer (to make the mail more interesting)

Adapting the Game

If you wish to use a mail game to introduce a visitor coming to your centre or home, just change the clue notes to suit your guest. You may want to play this type of game by having the child/children write back to the secret guest, or simply guess who is writing to them, even if the person is not coming for a visit.

Each area's postal system works differently. Ask the postal clerk how long a delivery will take, explaining the departure and destination points. Make a visit to your local post office.

DESIGNING YOUR OWN GAMES

mysteries and quests

Traditionally, mystery games require solving a "puzzle," involve crime and detection, or have an element of "spookiness," whereas "quests" usually have the flavour of an adventure– we are trying to reach a specific goal.

I always use a co-operative model; there is no winner, we all succeed. We always have an opponent such as time, a mythical figure, failure, or some dire consequence that has been set up in the context of the introduction.

The introduction to a mystery may last two minutes or two weeks. I usually introduce the game to the whole group at the same time, although one or two children may have found the initial clues which they excitedly share with the group. We then divide the whole group into smaller, more workable ones, and each follows a different path, achieving goals or collecting information, coming together again for the conclusion.

Each group, in its final stage, will find a piece of something (a map or a letter) which will require sharing information with the other groups in order to make sense of it all. This way, everyone reaches the conclusion together.

Be prepared for:

• The excitement that the game generates

- The children expanding on the ideas you present
- People wanting to know what you are doing (parents, principals, staff, other kids)

Be careful:

- Not to get caught up in overly-elaborate plans or props
- To use subject matter that will not offend or frighten the community you work with
- To have proper supervision during transitions (travelling from room to room or floor to floor)
- To set guidelines for behaviour during games, and have an alternative for children who cannot handle those guidelines
- To group the children in a way that spreads out skill levels and promotes co-operation

Getting Started

After using different logic puzzles and codes, you can start planning your quests and mysteries. Consult the game charts and clue lists for ideas, and use the guidelines for help in planning your mystery game or quest.

Decide on what type of role you want to play when a game is afoot. How many helpers will you need? Is it for a home birthday party, a classroom game or an after-school day-care setting? Do you wish to have a prize, a reward, a winner, or does everyone succeed?

Planning

It is better to have a short, small, successful quest than a long, complicated, incomplete one. It should work and you should always try it out first. Like a good joke, do not bother telling it if you are going to forget the punch line.

A quest or mystery game has four parts: a theme, an introduction, the process, and conclusion.

I have tried a variety of themes and styles of introduction (this is where a lot of the drama comes into play): creating a story around the game, letting subtle clues be found a week before the mystery begins, having odd things happen (all the chairs found upside down, or a symbol appearing in the playground) that no one will connect with the mystery until a story involving the symbol is found and read to the group.

Pick a theme or topic and plan it out (see chart). Consider:

Space– your classroom, your back yard, outdoors, halls, etc.

Time– for planning, for the introduction, for the process

Number of participants– how many groups, how many in each

Resources– other teachers, caretakers, other parents, props available

Planners' abilities– story-writing, art, acting

Mystery and Quest Planning Sheet

Theme _____ Setting _____

Time frame _____

Introduction _____

_____

# of participants _____ Age _____ # of groups _____

Groupings _____

Supervision required _____

Resources _____

Materials needed _____

_____

Process (Each group's path) _____

	Group A	Group B	Group C
Action 1			
Action 2			
Action 3			
Conclusion			
Evaluation			

Participants' abilities– reading skills, math skills, patience, attention span, independence levels

When you are planning, give yourself the freedom to use a variety of styles and to find the ones you feel confident in.

The conclusions of the games are the final reward; they can be events such as songs or dances that involve the whole group, or something material, like a new game or a toy. Try to make the game-playing worthwhile for its own sake, so that you are not just rewarding effort with treats.

Clues and Paths

1. Pick a method for leaving messages (for example, writing in glow-in-the-dark paint on clear plastic wrap)
2. Pick the type of message you want to leave (such as a scrambled-word clue)
3. Be creative with locations– try things like writing in mustard on a slice of bread or wrapping notes around toothbrushes.

The secrets to leaving good clues are making them exciting, and varying the amount of energy needed to figure them out. Some clues can be very straightforward (such as an arrow). Some clues may be useless to the game on the whole, but fun and exciting to see– footprints forming a trail, or a half-eaten cookie. Other clues may be part of figuring out the conclusion, such as parts of a map, pictures of "evidence," or decoding charts.

Write out each group's path by listing the group and its action. You may just have one path that is repeated by each group, or you may have three groups of children, each following a different path.

So look at some of the ideas presented, remembering you can always change them around.

Ways of leaving clues

- Hiding messages in balloons
- Writing in soap on mirrors or glass
- Writing in chalk on fabric that can be washed
- Writing in chalk on outside brick walls or pavement
- Writing in food colouring on bread slices
- Writing in washable markers
- Sticking paper cutouts onto walls
- Hanging fabric or paper banners
- Writing messages in glow-in-the-dark markers or paint on glass, windows or mirrors
- Writing in glow-in-the-dark markers or paint on clear plastic wrap to be hung up
- Taping messages
- Videotaping messages
- Mailing cards ahead of time
- Leaving messages on friends' answering machines (co-operation and timing important here)

- Arranging pennies on the ground to spell out words or look like arrows
- Using icing on cookies
- Leaving popcorn in the garden beds
- Planting sticks in the ground with flags
- Weaving pieces of cloth into a chain link fence
- Freezing small, laminated notes in ice cubes

Types of clues and paths

- Word scrambles
- Number codes
- Letter codes
- Sound codes
- Colour codes
- Backwards writings
- Reflection writings
- Lemon juice writings
- Letters cut out or carved into objects
- Messages on leaves
- Torn-up maps
- Torn-up messages
- Riddle clues

- Directional clues
- Physical challenges– such as ten push-ups, or running around the baseball diamond
- Related-object clues– such as toothbrush, face cloth and soap = bathroom
- Scratch-and-see clue cards
- Peel-and-see clue cards

Just to get you thinking, here are some of the game titles we played at Brant Street Daycare:

- Bear's Will
- Witches' Fingers
- Where's Bev?
- Space Aliens in the playground?
- Leprechaun Visit
- Rabbit Tracks
- Howling Wolf

You may have already been playing mystery games and quests and have found some of the games or riddles familiar. I hope some of these ideas are helpful or inspiring; perhaps they remind you of your own childhood and the feelings of discovery and adventure.

I would like to thank all the staff, kids and families at Brant Street Daycare, Alpha Alternative School, and Downtown Alternative School, for their contributions and for playing along. Especially my fellow "sneakers"

acknowledgements

Martha, Shamin, Nalini, Bev, Trudy, Ted, Judy, Beth and Kathy.

There are those who say you are only two people away from who you need to know… well, in this case it was three. My thanks to Noel Young, for inviting me to look out the window, and to John Fleming and Judy Diehl for helping me connect with the great people at Annick Press.

And last, but not least, thanks to my big brother Brad, for all the times he turned his bedroom into an elaborate haunted house, just to scare my friends and me. We loved it!